6.08

just lately I realise

Gate
HOUSE

Acknowledgements
Gatehouse Books Ltd is grateful for continued financial support from
Manchester City Council, Manchester Adult Education Service and North
West Arts Board and for financial assistance towards the publication of this
book from the Commission For Racial Equality and North West Arts
Board.
Gatehouse is grateful also to M.A.S.S. Rag (Manchester and Salford
Students' Rag) for a donation towards the 1993 edition.

Our special thanks are due to Emelda Walters, to Carole Whitehurst of
Longsight Reading Club and Fran Jackson, Judy Daborn and Judy Craven
of 8411 Community Education Centre, Moss Side, who helped by making
time and space available.

Published and distributed by Gatehouse Books Ltd
Birley Centre, Chichester Road, Manchester M15 5FU

Typeset in Univers series by Arena Design
Printed by L.V. Lawlor, Oldham
Reprinted 1986, 1993.

ISBN 0 906253 17 9

British Library cataloguing in publication data: a catalogue record
for this book is available from the British Library

Gatehouse is a member group of the Federation of Worker Writers and
Community Publishers.

Contents

Line Breaking

We have designed the book
to make it useful to people
who don't find reading easy.
Some stories
are broken into short lines like this,
so you can take a break
at a point that makes sense.

INTRODUCTION

This introduction was written by Cloeta, Roslyn, Wilbert, William and Victoria and also by Stella from Gatehouse.

In this book five people, women and men from the West Indies tell stories from their lives. Making the book they have faced painful memories from childhood and from their early years struggling to make their way in this country.

It all began with people gathered around a table. Their meeting was part of the discussion and writing that went into producing "Opening Time",. Gatehouse's pack about writing, and the planners of the pack Gillian Frost and Chris Hoy were involved at this time. They began by reading some writing from Write First Time*. The writing was called "Proud To Be Black" by Sheona. Afterwards they talked about Sheona's writing and about themselves. As people went on meeting, the talking and the writing flowed. Memories hidden for many years were shared. All of us, writers and Gatehouse workers thought the memories coming from the workshop deserved a wider audience, so now we would like to share them with you.

Some of the stories were spoken then written down in Tobagan or Jamaican English *because that's the way we speak and that's the English we know. Our story and the way we speak it belong together. We lose control if it get change because it no point thinking that it get change by we. Somebody else will have to do it. We think it sound good and we hope you do too.*

Each writer got their writing ready for the book working with Stella. We read and talked about the memories and made changes in some parts to make things clearer or to add new information. We were helped in this process by people from 8411 Community Education Centre, Moss Side, Manchester. They spent time reading and discussing the writing and meeting some of the writers. We would like to thank Asha, Danny, Florence, Maria, Ken, Patricia and Victoria. It was at this time that Victoria contributed her memories of coming to England to the book. As well as adding new information this provides a contrast with the other stories because they are written rather than spoken memories.

For Wilbert childhood memories are the most painful. *I want to write about my life history. What's been done to me. I never been knocked about, small thing not big set of thing done to me in this country. And I still getting through.*

For the other writers their struggle to make a life here was the most difficult time. *When we first come in this country in the fifties we was handle as if we's nobody, coloured people wasn't exist! As time goes on and somebody pick up this book to read they realise what people have gone through. We just want to be heard if we have a right point.*

*Write First Time is a three times yearly collection of writing from basic education students, in newspaper format. It was forced to stop publication in March '85 owing to non renewal of grant by the Adult Literacy and Basic Skills Unit. Back copies are available however. Please contact Gatehouse for further information.

I Been Through A Lot

Wilbert   *photo: Gatehouse Project*

Wilbert

IN TRINIDAD AND TOBAGO
My name is Wilbert Gordon.
I come from Trinidad and Tobago
I belongs to two island.

My schooling
When I went to infants school.
I didn't get all the learning from infants.
Then I move on to standard 1
because of my age,
I was too big for the infants.
I spent a few years in standard 1,
then I have to change school
and go to different district called Delaford
to live with someone
through my father
who live with a different woman.
Then I went there
and my father was taking no heed of me.
My father is called Thomas Gordon.
He wasn't interested in me,
in my schooling,
because of the woman.
When you're not their child,
they treat you bad
which I end up in court with this woman
through she did me very harmful things.

She got kid too.
At my time it was two boy and a girl.
I went there, making four.
You must expect, she must feel
hard feeling against me.
She wouldn't feel pleased
the man kid come to stay there with her.
The woman name was Pinny.

She did me very harmful things
One Sunday afternoon
while we was out in the yard playing
we was playing some kind of game
with marbles
and I was winning,
I can remember that.
And the woman kid, Pinny's kid
wanted back his marble
so we started fighting over the marbles.
A neighbour called,
"Pinny, Pinny,
Wilbert is beating up your child"
and Pinny called me inside the kitchen,
and what she do
first thing
she tie my two hands behind my back
and then she loose it
and she take it
and she hold it over the cooking fire

where she was cooking
until it burn
and make a big blister.
That's why we end up in court.
So after that she finish,
she take it off and she told me
to hold it myself
and I did, after she did it.
She call back the same neighbour and say,
"Come and see what Wilbert do,
he burn his hand".
She did this to try to prove
I did the burn myself.
I was small then, I was eight or nine years.
Pretty small.

My aunt come
I got an aunt
who live in the same district
which is called Delaford
so the same neighbour went
and told my aunt that Pinny burn my hand,
Wilbert hand,
over the cooking fire.
My aunt, when she heard,
she come and she take me away
and keep me by her.
So she went and get the police
and brought the police down

and the police look at my hand.
At the time they didn't make an arrest,
they take statement,
what happen with the hand
and I told them what happened,
that Pinny did it.

They take me back
But when they got to realise
Pinny and my father came
and take me back away from my aunt
and take me back home.

The court case come around
So the court case come around.
It was trying in Roxborough
so we have to walk
from Delaford to Roxborough
in the morning.
Well it's three miles away from Delaford.
So in the morning
they wake me up very early,
Pinny and my father,
because we got to walk.

What to tell the magistrate
On our way,
walking to Roxborough,
they was telling me

The bay near Roxborough   *photo: Anne Bolt*

what to tell the magistrate,
that I was boiling a crab
and the water pitch up from the pan
and burn my hand
and scalded my hand,
so if I didn't tell the magistrate
what they say, they will tell him I'm a bad boy
so make him send me away to some home.
You call it Borstal, we call it 'Dats'*.
My father told me that,
with the woman.
They were shielding theirself.
When I was small I didn't realise
and they put it in my head.
We reach Roxborough very early in the morning.
When we reach there it wasn't daylight
and they knock at a house, some relation home,
and we have a sleep there till morning.
They separate me from them
when we reach the door in the courthouse.
I can remember that.

The Courthouse went very quiet
When the case has been called
they called me up,
they take me in first
and the woman came in after.
I did tell the magistrate what they said,
''I was boiling a crab

*'Dats' is the local word for Dartmoor, a remand
home for boys.   14

They tell me what to tell the magistrate　　　　*photo: Anne Bolt*

and the water pitch up from the pan
and burn my hand".
You never experience it, you know.
I tell you,
the courthouse went very quiet that day.
Maybe, they knew that
they put that in my head, to say.
I said it like a recitation.
The case dismissed.
They have to say that.

Pinny and my father win the case
and I went back home with them.

The woman from Goodwood
When my mother heard about my burn
and she come and see my hand
she shed tears.
She try and get me back home to Spayside
and make I stay with one of my uncles
for a while.
Until one day
this woman from Goodwood,
came to Spayside
and was staying by the Pilgrim family.
The Pilgrim, they was middle class,
they wasn't poor,
because the father was an overseer on the road.
We used to be backwards and forwards
to the Pilgrim family.
So one of the Pilgrim daughter
told the woman from Goodwood about me.
I don't know what she said,
what she told them.
So in the afternoon
the woman, which is Mrs Princess Smith
from Goodwood
called me and asked me
if I want to come and live with her in Goodwood.
So I said "Yes"

Charlotteville, the next village to Spayside

photo: Anne Bolt

and she went and see my mother,
discuss with my mother,
and my mother said "Yes" to her
and so I went to Goodwood.

So very lonely
We went on the 3 o'clock bus
in the afternoon, to Goodwood.
When I reached there, to Goodwood,
and I looked around
and I couldn't see Spayside
I shed tears.
I cried all night
I want to go back home,
because it was so very lonely.
Kind of lonely spot.
And when you looked round for the next house
you maybe had to walk half a mile.
And when I look, I couldn't see Spayside
and I couldn't see the two little island
– Goat Island and Little Tobago out in the sea,
where the bird of paradise live.
I try to look for those two island
that's my mark you see,
and I can't see them
so I cried.
I want to go back home.
I missed home.
I was never able to go back
because they kept me.
I was young still.
I was ten years old.

Little Tobago where the bird of paradise live   Behind is Goat Island   photo: Anne Bolt

I pick up a bit of responsibility

When I went to Goodwood
Mr Charity Smith have cows and lots of lands,
lands below the road,
bound with the rocks and the sea,
lands above the road also,
bound with different people, neighbours.
Then he have lands in a place called Flagstaff
belonging to him.
He was a very independant man.
And he believe in doing farming,
growing, what we call provision,
you call it vegetables,
sweet potatoes, yam, bananas, plantain
all different sort.
Then I pick up a bit of responsibility.
I have to go in the pasture
in the morning,
milk the cows,
go in the afternoon
give them water
and change pastures.
All the work leave to me now,
looking after the animals.
Sometimes I have to go to the garden,
you call it farm,
and fetch water.
We didn't have no pipes in the yard.
You had to go to the river
To get water in buckets.

You had to go the river, to get water in buckets   *photo: Anne Bolt*

Mrs Smith came pregnant

I live with Mr Charity Smith
It's about 2 or 3 years
then his wife came pregnant.
Now I was looking after those cows
changing and milking.
One cow called Kate.
Kate was in calf.
He told me, when the calf born
it's going to be mine.
The cow had calf,
then he went back on his word.
He told me the first calf
got to be for his son,
and I looking after all the years!
I brought him good luck;
son born after me.
Well, what he got belongs to his son
but, he should give me a calf of my own,
and not go back on his word.
He give the son before me.
And all that must get me upset, you know.

I run away

So, I run away on a Sunday night.
He have a shop, a corner shop,
Sell cakes and sweet drink.
Whilst he was in the shop
with his wife and customers
I runned away.

On the Sunday night I stay by somebody,
and on the Monday morning
I went to the place called Delaford
which my father was living at
with the next woman.
The Monday afternoon when the bus coming up
Mr Charity Smith saw me on the road!
I was with the other kids,
playing on the road
and he stop the bus
and ask me where I'm staying.
I took him where I was staying by my father.
He told my father that I ran away from home
and he take me back to Goodwood
the following morning.
I was fourteen years old.

I get licks from them
Well still if I do anything wrong
I get licks from them.
He was cutting a twig from a tree
and then hold me in his hand
and give me about six or twelve lashes
on the back, if I do something wrong.
We didn't live in the village
so got to walk three miles to get to the school
in Goodwood Village.
If I am late from school
I used to get beat for that.

Hoeing sweet potatoes   *photo: Anne Bolt*

I thought I had to wait
One day he send me with a saw
to a place you call Monk St. George.
Well, I thought I had to wait
till the fellow sharpen the saw
and I wait for it.
When I got home, the man was home
and he didn't go to look after the cows.
He was home all day and he waited on me
to go and look at his cows.
When I come back I got belted
I couldn't sit down!
Then I have to go and look after the cows.

It was raining and muddy
and the cows wrap their chain
around all the tree stumps
I have to move them
and he's home, but he wouldn't go and do it.
So, he was getting too big for his shoes.

The only time I've been settled
Afterward I grown up.
I leave him through the bad treatment
and I went to different village
called Canaan and all those places.
I left there and went to Trinidad
to live on my own.
After I left Goodwood
I enjoy my growing up,
I have a lot of fun.
You see I have a bit of ups and down in life
and the only time I think I've been settled
is when I move to England.
I been hurt in my childhood, you know.
I been through a lot.
Sometime rejoicing, sometime not.
I think maybe I'm here
to go through some kind of punishment
because Jesus Christ used the word
he say something like, "I wouldn't bear
my cross alone. Somebody have to help me to
bear this cross".

So I think .... I been helping him
bear his cross,
and it's only now
I'm getting a bit of comfortable life.

I'm A Working Man

William   *photo: John Smith*

William

IN JAMAICA

My early life
I missed going to school.
My father died
when I was a little tot.
There were my mother
and nine of us.
So my father die
when I very small
so I never had to
go to school.
And then I wrote my uncle
and my uncle is a big farmer.
He grows coffee, sugar cane,
pineapple, chocolate,
we call it cocoa,
cocoa bean and pimento.

About pimento
Pimento is a very good thing.
It's a berry.
When it ripe
bird feed on it
and you break it
and put it in barbecue
and dry it.
Then you bag it up
and take it in town

and sell it
to the merchant.

Pimento is a seed
use in the army.
It season meat.
Very good for cooking soup.
It good for fever.
When it dry
go black like a berry.

Pimento berries   *drawing: Martin Fitzpatrick*

You get the pimento,
the dry pimento,
put it in a bottle
and throw some rum in it.
Very good in winter.
You rub your body with it.
It keeps you warm.
You put the berry in your shoes.
It keep your feet warm.
It is a very good thing.
My uncle have
two different place
where he grew his sugar cane
and he have about sixteen acres
in pasture
where he keep his mule,
and he have a lot of pimento.
Pimento grow on big trees
like apple trees
and pear trees.
When the berry ripe,
the bird feed on them.

About sugar cane
Sugar cane, that's hard work,
very hard.
You got to cut the cane
and bring it to the mill
and then

Sugar cane, that's hard work

photo: Anne Bolt

the horse or the mule
go around in a circle
and draw it
and the juice come out
into a barrel
and it go on the fire
and it boil.
It take seven tin of liquor
to a barrel
and in the month
of March and April
sugar cane is very sweet.
Then, seven tin of liquor
it give one tin of sugar
that is, sixteen quarts.

Rats and owls eat the crop
Rats and mongoose
eat the sugar cane.
It's very sweet,
very sweet.
You plant a lot of corn
and in the night,
rats eat the corn.
Owls screech in the night.
They go and feed
on the corn, as well.
Them go and feed
in the night

because them don't feed
in the day.
In the day
them hide in the trees
because those birds
can't see in the days.
They feed on the corn
and pineapple.

About pineapple
You have the sugar-pine,
you have cowboy-pine
and you have black-pine.
This is three different variety
of pineapple.
Sugar-pine and black-pine
is stout,
and the black-pine
is very stout.
You don't see the big ones
over here.
You see pineapple over here
but you don't see those.

Harvesting the crops
When the pimento come
my uncle employ people
to help to reap it,

and also the cane
and the coffee.
When it ripe
you got to pick it
off the trees
and pulp it.
You start reap on Monday
and you finish on Friday.
You pulp the coffee
Friday evening,
Saturday morning
you go to the river
and you wash it
and spread it out
in the barbecue
and leave it, get sun
and dry.
So you got to have
more than two hands
to help to get it
because coffee always reap
the month of October.
It always come in the rainy season.
Also pimento;
sometime you get it
in the rainy season,
June and July.
If you get rain
and you have

. . . You have the sugar pine   *photo: Anne Bolt*

five or six bags of pimento
you won't manage it.
If it don't dry
and the rain catch it,
it spoil.
Especially the pimento
because is a berry
and is easy to spoil.
If you put it down there
and it rain
and you bag it up,
it spoil.
You got to leave it out
and when the rain fall
and the water dry out
and the sun comes out
then it can dry it out,
it's alright.
But if you bag it up damp
it spoil.
It just rot away.
And with the coffee,
if you don't dry it properly
it get mouldy.
Mould grow on it
You have to get somebody
to help you with it.

With the coffee if you don't dry it properly it get mouldy.   photo: Anne Bolt

He only learn it from a book
Back in '51
an English bloke come to Jamaica
as a agricultural instructor.
He come to St. Thomas,
that's where I born and grow.
I work at a place in New Monkland
planting banana.
He come to tell us
how to plant banana.
He said, "Banana suppose to plant
three feet apart."
I say, "No".
He say, "Yes".
He'd just come out from England,
from the agricultural college.
So I took my machete
and chop a banana leaf.
He take his tape
and the banana leaf is six feet.
I say, "You want banana eight feet apart.
You get a good growth,
a good bearing".
And then he believe what I'm saying.
I show him the right way
but his way was wrong
for he only learn it from a book.
But I work on a farm,
that's my living.

So I took my machete and chop a banana leaf

IN ENGLAND

I came to England
In 1957.
Life was very different for me.
I will tell you something.
Near Bradford Road Gasworks
going up,
they have eighteen factory
on the left hand side,
and I take less than half an hour
and go up the eighteen factory
and no job.

There was a brick factory
on the left hand side,
and I go there one morning
looking for a job.
"Sorry, no vacancy."
"Sorry, we don't employ coloured here."

The first job I get
it was no good.
It was 2/6d an hour,
£6.02 a week.
And then a friend asked for me
at Matthew Swain Wireworks,
Oldham Road.
I was a driver's mate,
delivering goods.

. . . and I take less than half an hour, and go up the eighteen factory and no job

photo: Photosource

The Trueshine Factory
I went to Liverpool
one Tuesday morning
at Trueshine, a factory.
I was a driver's mate
and I get out from the cab,
took the sheet off the lorry
and the stacka-truck driver
came and pick up the first load.
He is the man that
when you go in the office
you give him the paper
and he check it
and after he take the load off
he sign, and you OK
and you can go back.
Well, he take the first load off
and then the buzzer blow.

The bloke who drive
the stacka-truck
he say, "OK, break."

Not getting served
When we went to the canteen
there's about six hundred
of us there,
and I'm the only one coloured
and they call a strike

just through me.
Everybody line up
and them all looking
looking round at me.
Everybody be looking and talking.
The stacka-truck driver,
he's a shop steward,
and he say to the whole canteen,
(excuse the language)
"That black bastard
not getting served here".

Everybody be looking and talking   photo: BBC Hulton Picture Library

There would be six hundred of us there.
I'm the only one coloured.
They call a strike.

My mate speaks up
Then my mate, the driver,
him name George, a white fellow, say,
"What happen, call the foreman".
And the foreman and the manager
them come up and ask, "What's wrong?"
And all the workers them say,
"That black bastard not getting served here."
Some big bloke down there.
Big and rough.
They do want to hit me.
George was stood by my side
and say to the foreman,
"No, he's my mate
and he's good as anybody else.
He's a driver's mate."
The foreman say,
"Alright, serve him."
The bloke who serving the tea
charge me 2/6d
for a cup of tea and a sandwich.
It was the wrong price.
He put more price on me.

He 'got' to do it

When we finish our break
and we came back to the load
I pull my cigarette out
and I give one to him,
the man who drive the stacka-truck
and he took it,
yes, he took it off me.
He said, "OK".
My mate said to him,
"What you done man?"

. . . and he took the cigarette, yes he took it off me.
photo: BBC Hulton Picture Library

He said well he got to do that
to suit his people
because if him don't call a strike
them throw him out of the union.
That place was called Trueshine.
No black guy work there.

What am I going to do?
We leave and come back to Manchester
and go in the yard.
The foreman ask George
how we get on, the first day.
So he explain
and tell him what happen.
The foreman say to George "Well he be going back
Thursday morning again.
He's the only one
that can go out with you."
I say to myself, "What am I going to do?"
You get in a job
you have to do it, for that's your job.
I come over here to work,
I used to work
I know about work
I'm a working man.
I have no education
All I want, to work,
to make my living
and that's it.

Back to Trueshine

And I went back there Thursday
and the same bloke,
who drive the stacka-truck
come to us again
to take the load off.
As soon as him take the first lift-off
again the buzzer went,
and my mate say to him,
"Can he have a drink this morning
without no strike?"
He say, "Oh yes,"
and he repeat what he said on Tuesday,
"I got to do it.
It's my job.
If I don't do it
they throw me out of the union
and I lose my job."
I been there about six time
and it's the same one bloke
we meet all the time.
Every time we go there
the first lift we take off
put it down,
the buzzer went
and we have to go to break.

Why don't you be alright?
I come in this country '57.
Around '58, '59, that happen to me.
If you leave your country
and go to a different country
you're looking for a honest living.
And you working with people
and you really say,
"Why don't you be alright?"
For it's true you know,
if English people
come to Jamaica
you look after them.
But when we came over here
it's a different tale.

My Experience Of England

Victoria

Victoria

We took a train to London   photo: BBC Hulton Picture Library

MY EXPERIENCE OF ENGLAND

This is about Britain after the war, when things were very bad and Britain needed people from all races and countries to come and work and help put the country right.

That's where I come in. I am from the West Indies. Things were bad in those days at home and in the paper you could read how England needed people to work in all fields. So my friend and I decided we would apply for a nursing job which we did, and got an answer to our application to come and take up a post. In those days you did not have to go to college or pass any 'O' level or exam for such a job. You could improve yourself as you go along.

Well in those days everybody travelled by boat and we arrived at Dover. We took a train to London and a taxi to Bethnal Green Hospital, only to find out that my friend and myself wouldn't be staying together. I was to go to the West Midland Hospital. That was my first disappointment, to split from my friend. Anyway I did not have any choice. I left London about 11 pm, reached Staffordshire in the early morning. On my way down I look outside now and then and saw smoke coming out of all the houses. In my mind I was thinking no wonder so many people are coming here, for at the time all those houses were factories to me, seeing smoke coming from them. I took a cab from the station to the hospital only to realise that the same factories were houses and where I am going to live. That was my second shock. In those days hospitals were not like they are now. Hard work and very little money. In the end everything got on my nerves. I could not stand the sight of blood and that was the end of my nursing. Well there was nothing else I could do but turn to the factory. To get a job elsewhere with my colour, not likely! Now I realise the mistake I made by coming here.

The start of my hardship

This was really the start of my hardship. I was on my own. Then another thing, I could not get anywhere to live. No one wanted to know. There were only a few black houses around and they were full top and bottom, four and six people to one room. At the hospital I shared a room with another girl. When I did get a place to live I had to share a room with two other girls. That I did not like as I was not used to living with strangers. At this time my friend in London was doing fine for people in London were more human and other black girls were in the hospital.

I did not want to send home to tell my family about

At the time those houses were factories to me, seeing smoke coming out of them.

photo: Alan Parkinson. Rentasnap.

my hardships. It was years after when I went home on a visit that the full story was told. How I had suffered hardship.

I did not tell my family how I had suffered hardship

photo: BBC Hulton Picture Library

My first Winter

Now I must tell you about my first winter. Things were not like they are now. The room was so cold, thinking about it now makes me shiver. The landlord was so mean that although three of us were sharing the one room, the little coal he gave us was just a handful. In that little room we had to wash out

54

clothes and dry them around the fire. In those days there was no wash house, no central heating, only coal and oil fire. We had no blanket on our bed. In those days blankets were for the rich and that would be army blankets. People that came here between fifteen to twenty years ago don't know what England looked like after the war because all the mess had been cleaned up and they arrived here seeing houses with fitted carpet, central heating, washing machines. Well-furnished houses. They don't know what we went through. No wonder why these younger generation treat things so badly, they don't know what we had gone through over the years. I must go back to myself; after my first winter, I started to look around to see if I could get a room for myself. No way did I want to go through the same thing again, another winter with three of us in one room. So I looked round and saw lots of rooms to rent, but little did I know these rooms were not for black faces. I walked till I gave up. There were no social services that you could go to for help. If you were out of a job not even dole money, for the long queue and waiting would break your spirit.

The things I told him!

Anyway I met a man who was to be my husband and we got married, for in those days to be on your own was no good and to live with a man was not respectable. To have my own room, the feeling was good. After a time my husband lost his job and we moved to Manchester. In those days everybody lived in Moss Side, I mean black people, and that was where you got all your contacts. This is something I must tell you. My husband came to Manchester before me and got this little room in the attic. I arrived in Manchester late the Saturday night so tired that I went straight to bed. I woke up the Sunday morning and wanted to make a cup of tea. As I did not see any kitchen I knocked on a door below me and asked the lady, "Where is the kitchen?" She turned her head with a smile and said, "See your kitchen there." She was referring to a stove on the stairs. So I asked her, "Where do I get water?" "In the bathroom", she said, "Also the toilet is in the bathroom". I was so mad, I don't know how I did not fall down the stairs. I asked "Where is the landlord?" "On the first floor," she said. The things I told him, thinking about it now makes me laugh!

Everybody seemed to know each other

Anyway in those days rooms were not hard to get, as a lot of black people had their own home. Denmark Road was the centre of activities with the market. Everybody seemed to know each other. Those were happy days. Not like nowdays with all these houses, the place looks like a concrete jungle. I remember

Denmark Road was the centre of activities, with the market

photo: Photosource

the great shops on Alex Road which were pulled down.

It is funny how some times you can think back on the years that pass. The other day on my way to Birmingham I remembered all those little houses with smoke coming out of them. The place doesn't look the same any more, with all those motorways and sky-high buildings.

My working days here

I must tell you about my working days here. When I came here there wasn't much money around. We lived on next to nothing, saving every penny we could put our hands on to buy our own house and to make two ends meet. It was very hard on us then.

I am retired and looking back on my working days now. Sometimes I wonder if things could be better than the way they were, when we were slaving away with the work. I did machining for some years and that factory was so cold that thinking about it now makes my blood run cold. I did piece work for a while and I was glad when I was taken off it, for in my opinion I think it was wrong for anyone to work in such conditions. After I came off piece work the work was very interesting. I was making coats and love doing so. The girls were all nice to work with. I do miss going to work. I just imagine with half of the country out of work now, how they all feel. To keep me active I go to day and evening class and I think it is very good. I would advise anyone who is out of work to try and find something to do. There are lots of things going on these days free that you could fit yourself into. So don't stay at home and make yourself miserable and fed up. Don't forget, God blesses those that help themselves.

I Just Take It

Roslyn

IN JAMAICA

When I was a child in Jamaica I did not grow up with my mother and father. Them gave me away to a pair of people, Mr and Mistress Whitely, and them did not send me to school. Them have me from I was about four years old and all I did was work. One day I looked and see the children was coming from school and I ask the woman I was with why I am not going to school. She tell me that she is not my mother so I tell her that I wanted to go home to my mother and I started to cry.

Going home

About three weeks after, one morning she said that she is sending me home. At that time I was twelve years old and straight as I go to my mother she was so shocked to know that I was not going to school till she started to cry and she send me to school now. But that time I was so big and old that I did not want to go. I was so ashamed that I did not want to stay in school now. Anyway I go for a little time and through that, I did not get to learn the way I should. When I leave school I could not read and write the way I would like.

*One day I look and see the children coming
home from school*   photo: Lennox Smillie, Camera Press

IN ENGLAND

Meeting with prejudice

When you are in Jamaica and didn't know about this country, everybody would be happy to come here. From the time you hear about England and everybody going to England you going to make a try to go too, to see what the difference. To see what England is like. Well, now I travel, I do not regret it because things that I experience and gathered now, if I was at home I wouldn't gather that much but the way they treat you, it's terrible. In those times when I first came here you didn't need much education to get a job, but when you do get the job they treat you terrible. I don't know if it's true for everyone, but it's true for what I go through and see. It was terrible for me. I can remember many days I sit down and cry and I said I don't know why they behave this way in this country to coloured.

Roslyn just before she left Jamaica

No Vacancies

When I first come in this country I go to the labour to get a job. Them sent me to a job, but from the manager look out and see that I was black, right away him say sorry to me, he did not have any vacancy, so I went back to the labour and tell them what the manager say. The labour man went and phoned up to find out why them did not give me the job, but them did not tell him why.

So you see that we coloured go through a lot of things in this country. What the white will do and get away with it the black can't do it, and if black and white go to look for a job, the white will get it and the black not.

Sometimes I wonder why, what is the difference, some white is so loving and friendly and some is not. Before I come to this country, if somebody did tell me "When you go there they will be prejudiced against coloured", I say "no", until when I come I see it for myself and it is true.

I get a job

When I first get a job it was in a mineral factory washing bottles to put the mineral in and it was very cold. Sometimes when I hold the bottle my hands go

63

numb and I have to go and put them in hot water to get life in them back. One day I went to work and the manager tell me, "You must keep to your own people". It was four black work there.

"No wages for you"

When I first started to work there I can remember I took sick and went off. And when I went back to work one of the workers say to me, "There won't be any wages for you so don't bother to wait in the queue". So I got my things and I went. I wait for another girl who's getting her wages. Shortly after she came to me and she said, "There was some tax rebate there for you, you know. Your name called for it!" So I said, 'Right, I'll get it tomorrow then'. Then I went home. Go back to work on Saturday morning. When I went to the timekeeper and ask him for it he said, he send it back to the tax office so I'll get it on Monday. Well, I didn't go back on Monday to ask for it. I think if they have it for me I shouldn't have to go for it since they know I'm at work so I wait until Friday when I go for my other wages. I ask for it, he said, no, I work, so I wouldn't get it again. It was the timekeeper. He was the one, who kept it for himself.

Down in the cellar

I worked there for about 9 months. At the end part it was very terrible. I was expecting a baby and I didn't

It was the timekeeper, he was the one who kept it for himself

photo: BBC Hulton Picture Library

tell the manager and them put me down in a deep cellar taking the bottles from the ground and packing them up on top. It made me ill and I go home. I didn't tell the doctor what was happen, but he wouldn't send me back to work because I was rather poorly and he send me to the hospital. I think that I have a hernia.

Laying off people

When I went back to the mineral factory after the baby they said there wasn't any vacancy for me there. So I go back to the labour. Labour man said, "Your job supposed to be there". They phone up the factory but the mineral factory wouldn't gave it back to me. They say it was summer and they were laying off people. I didn't know why they say it. It's just lately I realise what was happening.

When I first get a job it was in a mineral factory

photo: Nick Hedges

Sharing Feelings with the Group

As trust built up within Roslyn's group, the bitter experience of racial prejudice which had soured the working lives of all but one of them came to the surface. What follows is a conversation between Roslyn and Emelda about how you cope at work. Emelda is a younger woman than Roslyn and it's interesting to note the difference in attitudes.

Roslyn

ROSLYN
If I'm at work, I don't make trouble with anybody. If anybody try to upset me, and if I feel rather embarrassed at what them say, I went to the toilet and have a cry. I come back and I sit down and what I'll do then I won't talk to that person. I'll just leave them.

Emelda

EMELDA
I mean, you could only take so much though. I could understand not wanting to fight management, but after you'd been in the place say five or six years, you could have started giving the workers back some of what they gave you.

ROSLYN
You can have a quarrel and things like that, but if you fight they sack you. If it's two of you is coloured fighting, it's probably different because they might sort out the two of you. They'll talk to you and probably not tell the manager. But if it's another white, you don't have a job.

When I was working at a potato crisp factory, a girl took a chair from a white. The girl had the chair but she keep it for somebody else and there is this white woman come and take it and the black girl decide to get it back. They saw her between two chair and they sacked her, they sacked the coloured. But the union was there and the union step on it and they had to take her on back. But in those things I wouldn't want to go back, you see. If they sack me it worries me and then the union have to compel them to take me back. I wouldn't go back. I'd feel rather embarrass to face them again. I try just to make nobody have anything to say about me. I take it for so long.

EMELDA
You never had an argument with anybody?

ROSLYN
No matter what them doing I don't answer.

EMELDA
You'd have to hear my voice. You've got to fight back sometime.

ROSLYN
Well I had a friend. Both of us used to work together

and sometime she come to me and said, "It's because you're soft, white people have to walk on you". She will butt in and I say "Right, leave it alone". I don't like embarrassment. I don't want to get in contention. I don't talk much unless I'm on my own with the kids.

EMELDA
I used to feel bad when my mam was talking about work. Sometime she'd be dead upset and quiet and I'd feel how come, how can they talk to my mother like that? How can they treat her like that? That's my mother. She goes out daily to earn us some bread, work very hard in terrible conditions and then to be treated like that. I used to be very resentful. I'd say "Leave the job, leave the job". That's what I used to tell her, "Go find something else".

ROSLYN
My kids are telling me the same thing.

Twelve machine to run

When I first started to work at the potato crisp factory everybody was gone on holiday because June to August they always Manchester holidays, and if you

71

happen to work during those week you all got to help doing all that job. We had twelve machine to run between two of us. They are very far apart and you got to do them. I can remember one day it was me and a white girl working, only two of us on the line, twelve machine six machines each, and believe me I don't think my partner stirred once in five minutes. I alone along that line, backward and forward, backward and forward on those twelve machine, and I get so tired and weary I don't think I could cope with it any longer and I decide to turn off the six at the top and the line forelady came down and she put the six of them back on and she say, "Look now Flowers, I want these six machine to run and don't you turn them back off". I said "Well Norma, it's me alone. I haven't seen Ann. Where is she?" She say "That have nothing to do with me. I want them to run". If it was Ann tell her that I am missing, she would have found me anywhere in the place, anywhere I may be, and if it was Ann tell her that, she wouldn't come and tell me that Ann say I've gone. But I said that to her and she go and tell Ann in the rest room, that I am complaining outside, that she left me on my own, and then Ann come out and started to get mad. And they went away and they'll go and sit down and have a cup of tea and have a chat while I work.

EMELDA
And you didn't say anything. Oh God! You deserve a halo!

ROSLYN
Saying anything, where would I go? If I go to the office they going to say "No, it didn't happen", because if I go to the office to report, that mean I report Norma which she is a forelady, and the whole lot of them would throw me through the door and this time I wouldn't be alive. I probably wouldn't have a job. There are people like this whenever time things go wrong, and especially if you is black, they really take it out of you. Them find all way to get at you so since I know that and I have proved it, it doesn't matter. I just take it.

EMELDA
But you could have killed yourself. You could have slipped on that floor, you could have hurt yourself trying to operate all those machines.

ROSLYN
And all those times if you slip and meet an accident you have nothing to get.

EMELDA
Yes that's it. You were tearing up and down that room, trying to get twelve machines going. Oh God no! I'd rather switch the damn machines off or leave, walk out or something because you can only go so far.

ROSLYN
Well the white would walked out, anyone of them would walked out but they come back tomorrow and they had them job but you or me walked out, we don't come back in there for a job.

Colour don't come nowhere

ROSLYN
They was looking for people for chargehand. They find out the whites who want to take the job. They don't come and say, "The longest worker in there will get it", they go to the line forelady or the line foreman and ask them who **they** think is the fittest one to be a chargehand and all of them – three shifts, all them that have put a A to your name, you will get it. One of the chargehand one day he talk about me, which I hear because he know me not making any trouble, and the line forelady said, "Colour don't come nowhere in this factory". The only colour will get a promotion in that factory must be a coloured that

74

born and grow here and go to school here and have so many 'O' levels and things like that. They can come anywhere in that factory, but other from that no coloured come nowhere. It's true, no coloured apply for nothing inside there and get it.

EMELDA
The thing what I can't understand, is that you wouldn't put up with those conditions in Jamaica. I mean people treating you badly, you wouldn't put up with them.

Here things are different

ROSLYN
Oh, no! But here things are different. Sometimes when you look around and see there's only one or two coloured among so many white, you can't do anything. You might want to try to volunteer for chargehand but there's no point in volunteering when you don't have a backer. I felt it, I got to say that. Plenty would say it does not happen but if things don't happen to you, you can't talk about it. I never really tell anyone what happen to me. Sometime I come home, I'm so embarrass I don't tell my husband anything because he probably go to the factory and make trouble. He don't put up with anything, he don't stand for it. If you say to him "Move that table!" and him feel like him not going to

move it, him tell you bluntly him not moving it. If you say "You **got** to move it", well he going to say, "Look if you know you got to move it, you move it yourself". Yes, he's like that. And if you tell him, "You're sacked. Through that door", he's gone and gone.

EMELDA

Once you shown people that you've got feeling, rather than just put up with everything and not respond, I think then they respect you a bit more. They think twice before they say things to you, whereas if you just let them walk all over you, they will!

A crisp factory in the 1960's.

He would have fight the bloke

ROSLYN
One time a line foreman at the factory hit me and I didn't come home and tell my husband. It was later he found out, when we went to this dinner party from the factory.

EMELDA
Oh you went to the work's do did you? I wouldn't have gone. There's no way they would have got my money.

ROSLYN
Well that foreman had left at the time.

EMELDA
Well, under any circumstances I wouldn't have gone to any of the functions. I would have just gone in and done my eight hours and that's it.

ROSLYN
Well this line foreman went to the work's do. Me and my husband was sitting in the bar. I was showing him, "That bloke is the one who hit me at work!" My husband started to swear and say "Now, you are telling me now!" Yes, he would have gone to the factory and he would have fight the bloke if he catch him. And being I know, I don't want any trouble, I

don't tell him anything, anything I know will bring trouble.

EMELDA
But that must be hard for you to keep things to yourself.

ROSLYN
Yes, well I did all the while.

EMELDA
I think a lot of women do. I mean not just black women, I think women generally keep things to themselves.

ROSLYN
Yes, plenty I would say. Not coloured women alone don't like trouble. You got plenty white don't like trouble and they'll do anything for peace. Or you have some of the awkward one, just like some of we coloured is the awkward one.

It's hard, because sometime you think about it. Keep saying to yourself what have you done, why such and such a thing had to happen to you, what can you do about it? Sometime I want just to pack my job in. Many the day I think about it. Then I say: "Why should anybody run me and force me to leave whose worked there so long?" Then I say to myself,

"I'll keep my word and keep my speech but they'll have to sack me. I won't take my cards".

And they think that you is dirt. When they look upon you and call you a black bastard. Oh yes, it's terrible. Oh yes, they call you a black bastard. It gets into your bones and sometimes you get fired up. It's just best not to bother.

EMELDA
What about your kids?

ROSLYN
Oh they don't take anything. I had three girls and one boy. The boy is just like him father. He doesn't trouble you but other than that he won't take no for an answer. Bernice she's just like me, she don't make trouble, but the other two girls they won't stand very much.

Angry

Form B

HOME OFFICE
application for registration as a
British citizen

on the grounds of ordinary residence
and/or relevant service or employment

British Nationality Act 1981 - Section 7
Applications are subject to time limits - see pages 6, 8 and 9 of the guide

IMPORTANT: Please read the guide enclosed with this form before you fill it in. Fill in the parts that apply to your application *(see page 10 of the guide)* **and cross out the other parts. If there is not enough space for your answer, use a separate sheet of paper. Please write in BLOCK LETTERS and use black or blue-black ink.**

WARNING: To give false information on this form knowingly or recklessly is a criminal offence punishable with up to 3 months imprisonment or a fine not exceeding £1000 or both
(Section 46 (1) of the British Nationality Act 1981).

1 Please give here date and Home Office **reference number** of any previous application or correspondence.

2 Surname/Family name — Mr/Mrs/Miss

All other names

Name at birth
if different from above

Date of birth

Place and country of birth

3 If name at birth is different from your present name please give

date of change
to present name

reason for change
(eg marriage, adoption, deed poll)

4 Present address

Daytime telephone number

Home telephone number
(if different)

Please report any change of address or telephone number

Victoria

ANGRY

Now listen to what nearly takes my breath away from me and lets me nearly drop dead.

After living here all these years I, as a good citizen, never got into any trouble. Now I hear that I am no more a British subject unless I register. I have lived here over 30 years. I came here with a British passport. At home before I came here, I lived British, slept British, walked British, went to school to learn to read and write all about England, the great country. I am retired now and I find I must go and buy my stay. If I want to live here I will have to go and register to be British. Something is wrong here, or people have become heartless. Is it fair to us? We who have lived here all these years, helped clean up the place and put Britain back on its feet? No, it is an insult to us and it is only black people this treatment is handed out to. All I can say is that black people are here to stay and the Government of this country can start getting used to living with us.

Hear My Voice ....
The Hardship Of Life

Cloeta

IN JAMAICA

My name is Cloeta.

I was born in Jamaica and my mother was very poor so I grow up with a step-mother. She treat me very bad. She did not send me to school. Most of the time she learn me to do gardening and most of the time to fetch water. Some times I go to school just one day of the week. It just one Saturday I go to the market and there was a lady said to me "Who is your father?" and I told her, so she said she will tell my mother for me, and in two weeks time my mother came for me and take me home.

Shame to go back

I was twelve years old when my mother took me back to school and I was so shame to go back just in A class, so I did not go back. But when I grow up I realise about my future. My future was so bad, was so sad. Anyway, I have got a job so I began to work so that I could help my mother and father and that was where my life started for a few more years. Then I met my future husband, I was engaged for three years, then I got married.

IN ENGLAND

My husband came to England in March 1962 and I came in August 1962 and I started to work 5th October at a cotton mill. I work for ten years and nine months, the reason for leaving, the cotton was getting onto my chest. At that time when I leave that job, I've got another job at Edwards the butchers, and I've worked there for 4 years.

The 'Pre-Tops' Course

I met a friend while I was working at Edwards. This friend sent me to North Hulme College to see the Headmaster and he explained everything about the course to me. So I went back and gave up my job. I started the course, it was very good*. I got my wages every week on Tuesday. I attended school every day for one year. When the end of the terms was up, I had to take a maths test. When I take the test I was very nervous that day when I take it. But at last I was glad for I had passed my test.

My troubles began

One month later I went to Salford College. In my first week there they learn us to make bread. Then on my

Cloeta setting out for England

second week all my troubles began when they sent me to do survey and all the recipes to write down. I didn't know I had to go through all that. I thought they was going to show us the practical things what to do. But they didn't do that. They just sit over there and tell you the recipe. You had to write down like 'A pound and a half of sugar' and 'Half a pound of butter and marzipan' so and so. It's a very big class and they just told you what to do and I couldn't cope with it.

I leave the school

I went back and explained to the Head Teacher so he wrote this letter for me, so that I could get back the money what I've spent. I spend about £58 because at that time I bought all my things – some cake decorating books, the uniform, the pinafore, towels and hand towels and everything, preparing to do the catering course.
So I leave the school and my sister got a job for me. But I still go to the night school, it is very useful to me. I am still going, now I am learning dressmaking.

Working at a drinks factory

I work at a drinks factory for seven years. This is the last job that I've had. There I was a machine operator, when I see what was going on when the new girls started. The forelady learn them to operate every part of the machine. I have to do all the dirty work at the back of the machine. It is three black woman working there. One day I asked the forelady why she never learn us other part of the machine, she told me that the young ones them don't like to work at the back of the machine. But why should we stay at the back all the time? So the trouble began.

We complaining!

That is when I started to complain. Then all the other rest of us started to said, "We complaining". They started to call us black b....... When we heard them our problem started. It was seven hard years of my life. So the next week the forelady started to move us around so we could do the job properly, so the girls, they started to shout at us, when they are showing us what to do. When we doing the job, if just a little is missed off or anything goes wrong, the linesman will come to us and he will start shouting. I said to him "Why you don't shout at the rest of them, why are you shouting at me like that?" So we had a quarrel. He told me, "If you cannot do the job you must go home". I was upset about it. So I tell him, "I am going to complain about you".

They are colour prejudiced

I went upstairs to see the manager and then I told him all that was happening downstairs. I was so mad that the manager told me to sit down for a few minutes because I couldn't talk. I told him, "They are coloured prejudiced", so he told me "It is not". One month after, the sign was up that the drinks factory was going to close down. I was sorry that the place was closing. So one day the same linesman said to me, "The place is closing down. What are you going to do?" I told him, "We are all going up the road now".

GOING BACK TO JAMAICA

I would like to go home because my husband is retired now and he becomes a pensioner. I also am not working now and I don't know if I will be able to get another job so I'm looking forward to see if I could go back home. I've made a start already and I've tried to make a quick move because things in this country now are getting from bad to worse and it's not so good. Job is very hard to get and at my age.

It would be different in Jamaica because if I go home now, I won't be working any more. Since I came here I've been working and all my life I been working all the time, so if I go home now I would just look forward to be a house wife and to enjoy my life.

Life will have changed in Jamaica

Life will have changed in Jamaica since I was there. Since that – 20 years ago life was better in Jamaica but its several years ago now since the politics was going on in Jamaica. When the corruption was

Cloeta and husband

going on there was a lot of people going away, coming out to go to Canada and America. Now things is gone back to normal, people is going back home. There are a few friends of mine that went on holiday and they said things is much better out there now. Also some friends had gone for good and they wrote back to me and said things is quite nice back here, hurry up and come home. I had a lot of relatives there. So I'm really looking forward now, soon.

Getting accustomed to the differences

Living there now, I don't think it would bother me much. I need a rest and I have to go back there now and get accustomed to the weather. Such as, we here now in England, we have on jumpers and vests and cardigan. We can't just go back and take them off right away. We have to take our time and take each one off each day, you know, as the day go along. We'll have to just try and do that. There might be certain fruits there now which you can't eat it right away also.

A better life

I'd like to live a better life. I've lived abroad for 20 years. As you go old, each day your body becomes a bit weaker and you have pains in your joints. I'm having rheumatism in my knees and I think it's the dampness of the weather. Since I'm not working now and my husband is retired, if we can get out of the cold weather I think it's best for us. Because the longer you is here, the worse it getting. A lot of people here want to go back. They wanted to go but they can't afford the money.

Kingston today   *photo: Lennox Smillie, Camera Press*

I would definitely have to get a house before I will get there because we have a lot of things to take home and see. There's a lot of people here as can go back home to relatives but as soon as they get there they need somewhere for themself. You don't want to go back home and be living at somebody place. You like to go back home and live independent. That's the reason why the majority of people they still here.

It's different with children

It's different for people with children. My sister had four kids born here and they doesn't want to go back home to live. She took the last one to Jamaica in 1983 to show her what Jamaica is like. She came back and said she didn't like Jamaica at all, and she doesn't want to go there. So if you had made your mind up to go home you'd just have to leave the kids behind. They won't like it.

Cloeta's Course

This is a course funded by the Training Services Division (TSD) of the Manpower Services Commission (MSC). Its aim is to improve job prospects by attempting to bring Maths and English up to a standard which will enable students to go on to further training or into employment. Cuts have led to drastic reductions in the number of courses and also in the length of the course ... from 36 weeks to 13 weeks.

Gatehouse Books

Gatehouse is a unique publisher

Our writers are adults who are developing their basic
reading and writing skills. Their ideas and experiences make
fascinating material for any reader, but are particularly
relevant for adults working on their reading and writing skills.

The books that come from Gatehouse are the work of people
whose stories, though worth the telling, would not normally
get into print.

Gatehouse books reflect back to the adult learner reader,
insights and experiences from other adult students. They
work because often the writing strikes a chord - a shared
experience of struggling against many odds.

The format of our books is clear and uncluttered. The
language is familiar and the text is often line-broken, so that
each line ends at a natural pause.

Gatehouse books are both popular and respected within
Adult Basic Education throughout the English speaking
world. They are also a valuable resource within secondary
schools, Special Needs Education, Social Services and
within the Prison Education Service and Probation Services.

They are a bond between writer and reader.

A promise that your story is worth telling too.

A stimulus for more student writing.

Booklist Available

For an up to date catalogue and details of other Gatehouse publications, please contact:

Orders
Gatehouse Books
Birley Centre
Chichester Road
Manchester M15 5FU

Tel: 061 226 7152

A donation of £1.00 towards the cost of the catalogue and postage would be appreciated. An invoice can be supplied for this if required. This would automatically add your name and address to our mailing list for new titles and future catalogues.

The Gatehouse Publishing Charity is a registered charity, reg. no. 1011042.

Gatehouse Books Ltd is a company limited by guarantee, reg. no. 2619614.